SKI
PATROLLER

BY CHRIS BOWMAN

BELLWETHER MEDIA · MINNEAPOLIS, MN

Are you ready to take it to the extreme?
Torque books thrust you into the action-packed world
of sports, vehicles, mystery, and adventure. These books
may include dirt, smoke, fire, and dangerous stunts.
WARNING: read at your own risk.

Library of Congress Cataloging-in-Publication Data

Bowman, Chris, 1990- author.
 Ski Patroller / by Chris Bowman.
    pages cm. -- (Torque: Dangerous Jobs)
 Summary: "Engaging images accompany information about ski patrollers. The combination of high-interest
subject matter and light text is intended for students in grades 3 through 7"-- Provided by publisher.
 Audience: Ages: 7-12.
 Audience: Grades: 3 to 7.
 Includes bibliographical references and index.
 ISBN 978-1-62617-113-8 (hardcover : alk. paper)
 1. Skis and skiing--Vocational guidance--Juvenile literature. 2. Ski patrollers--Juvenile literature.
 3. Hazardous occupations--Juvenile literature. I. Title.
 GV854.315.B68 2014
 796.93--dc23
                            2013050515

This edition first published in 2015 by Bellwether Media, Inc.

Printed in the United States of America, North Mankato, MN.

TABLE OF CONTENTS

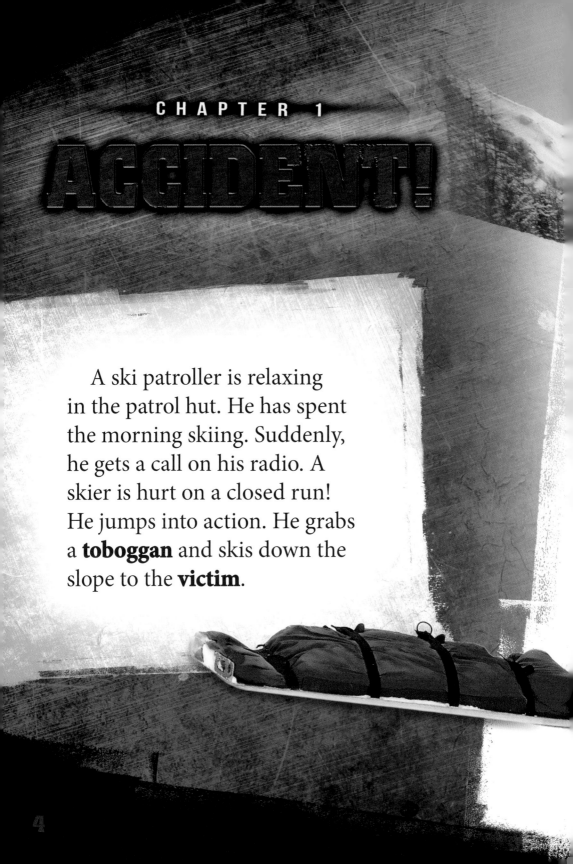

CHAPTER 1
ACCIDENT!

A ski patroller is relaxing in the patrol hut. He has spent the morning skiing. Suddenly, he gets a call on his radio. A skier is hurt on a closed run! He jumps into action. He grabs a **toboggan** and skis down the slope to the **victim**.

Other patrollers arrive at the scene. They strap the injured skier into the sled. A strong wind whips across the slope. Blowing snow makes it hard to see. The run is also icy. The patrollers ski slowly to make it down safely. An ambulance waits at the bottom of the mountain. Everyone is safe thanks to the ski patrol!

CHAPTER 2
SKI PATROLLERS

Ski patrollers make sure people stay safe out on the slopes. Patrollers are expert skiers or snowboarders. They work for **resorts** and patrol their runs. It is their job to help injured skiers. They may also take away **lift tickets** from those who are being unsafe.

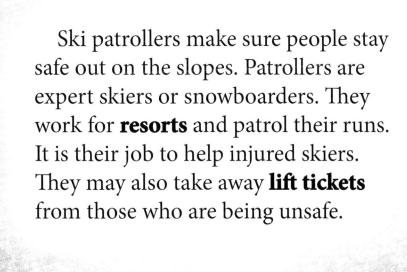

Humble Beginnings

The National Ski Patrol was formed in the United States in 1938. Charles Minot "Minnie" Dole formed a small patrol for a downhill ski race. He later made a national patrol.

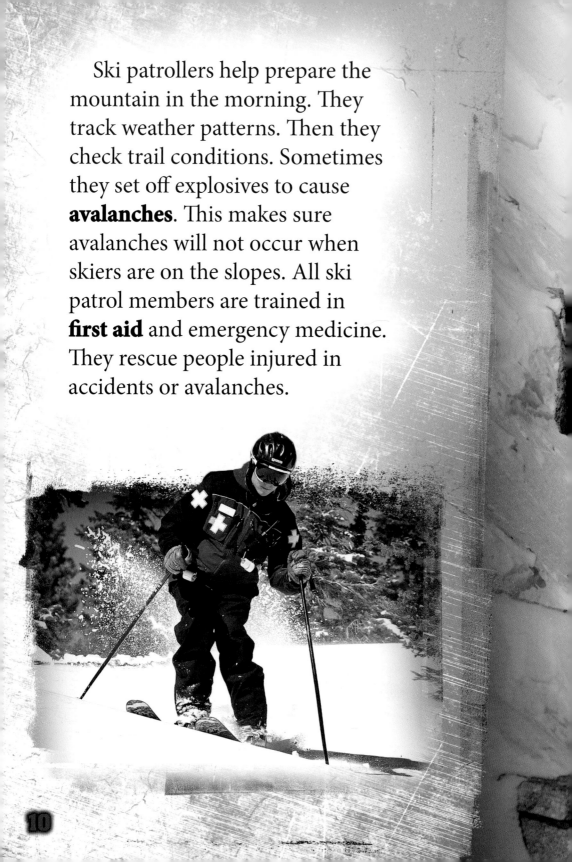

Ski patrollers help prepare the mountain in the morning. They track weather patterns. Then they check trail conditions. Sometimes they set off explosives to cause **avalanches**. This makes sure avalanches will not occur when skiers are on the slopes. All ski patrol members are trained in **first aid** and emergency medicine. They rescue people injured in accidents or avalanches.

Lift Off

Patrollers are also trained to rescue people from chairlifts if the power fails.

Patrollers have an active job that requires physical fitness. They load and move injured skiers. They pull them on sleds. Patrollers must be able to ski any run on the mountain with a sled behind them. Search and rescue duties can also be physically demanding.

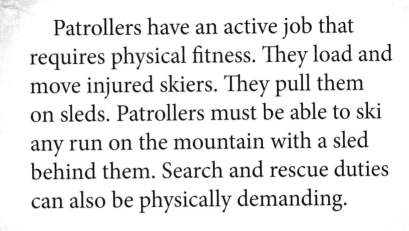

Friendly Helpers

Some patrollers have trained dogs that help them search for avalanche victims. Snow rescue dogs use their noses to find people under the snow.

Ski patrollers model mountain safety. They need a lot of gear for this. They dress in layers to stay warm. Helmets and goggles protect their heads and eyes. They carry first aid kits and radios. On rescues outside of the resort, patrollers bring **probe poles**, shovels, and **beacons**.

CHAPTER 3

DANGER!

Ski patrollers are prepared to take all kinds of risks. Getting injured in a crash is always possible when skiing or snowboarding. Sometimes rescues take patrollers to unsafe areas, including the **backcountry**. Rough terrain and changing weather conditions are common dangers.

In the Wild

Many ski patrollers will leave the resort to help in the backcountry. There, rescues are always risky because snow conditions can change quickly.

In extremely cold temperatures, patrollers risk **frostbite** and **hypothermia**. They may need to patrol slopes during winter storms. They also chance getting caught in an avalanche. Patrollers are trained in avalanche control and rescue. However, avalanches occur with little warning. Only about one in four avalanche victims survives.

Get Some Air

Many patrollers have airbag packs. These backpacks inflate to keep them close to the surface in an avalanche.

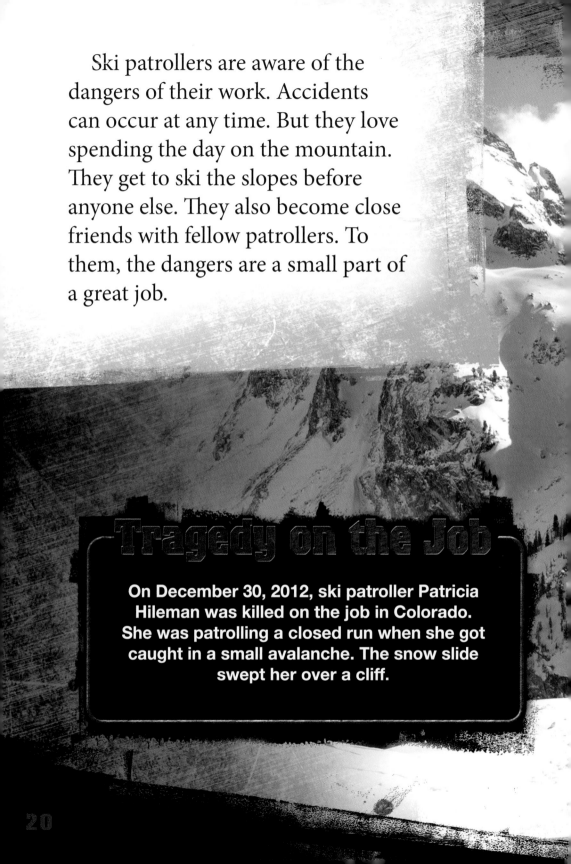

Ski patrollers are aware of the dangers of their work. Accidents can occur at any time. But they love spending the day on the mountain. They get to ski the slopes before anyone else. They also become close friends with fellow patrollers. To them, the dangers are a small part of a great job.

Tragedy on the Job

On December 30, 2012, ski patroller Patricia Hileman was killed on the job in Colorado. She was patrolling a closed run when she got caught in a small avalanche. The snow slide swept her over a cliff.

Glossary

avalanches—massive snow slides

backcountry—ungroomed or unmarked slopes; the backcountry lies outside of a ski resort.

beacons—devices that send out radio signals; beacons help patrollers find people buried in avalanches.

first aid—emergency medical care given to a sick or injured person before he or she reaches a hospital

frostbite—a condition in which the body tissues are damaged by extreme cold

hypothermia—a condition in which the body loses heat faster than it can produce it; hypothermia causes body systems to shut down.

lift tickets—passes that show that skiers paid to ride a chairlift up the mountain

probe poles—long, light poles that can be extended down into the snow to find people

resorts—vacation spots that offer recreation, entertainment, and relaxation; ski resorts offer hills for winter sports such as skiing and snowboarding.

toboggan—a sled

victim—a person who is hurt, killed, or made to suffer

To Learn More

AT THE LIBRARY

Burns, Kylie. *Alpine and Freestyle Skiing.* New York, N.Y.: Crabtree Pub. Co., 2010.

Champion, Neil. *Wild Snow: Skiing and Snowboarding.* Mankato, Minn.: Smart Apple Media, 2013.

Green, Sara. *Snow Search Dogs.* Minneapolis, Minn.: Bellwether Media, 2014.

ON THE WEB

Learning more about ski patrollers is as easy as 1, 2, 3.

1. Go to www.factsurfer.com.

2. Enter "ski patrollers" into the search box.

3. Click the "Surf" button and you will see a list of related web sites.

With factsurfer.com, finding more information is just a click away.

Index